Motor Racing at
Oulton Park
in the 1960s

Peter McFadyen

VELOCE PUBLISHING
THE PUBLISHER OF FINE AUTOMOTIVE BOOKS

Also from Veloce Publishing -

First published in September 2006 by Veloce Publishing Limited, 33 Trinity Street, Dorchester DT1 1TT, England. Fax 01305 268864/e-mail info@veloce.co.uk/web www.veloce.co.uk or www.velocebooks.com
ISBN 1-84584-038-0/ISBN 13: 978-1-84584-038-9/UPC: 636847-04038-3

Readers with ideas for automotive books, or books on other transport or related hobby subjects, are invited to write to the editorial director of Veloce Publishing at the above address.

British Library Cataloguing in Publication Data – A catalogue record for this book is available from the British Library. Typesetting, design and page make-up all by Veloce Publishing Ltd on Apple Mac.
Printed in India by Replika Press Pvt.

Contents

Foreword & acknowledgements

Foreword

I first visited Oulton Park in the 1950s, when the circuit was but a few years old and I was not much older. Having to depend upon my father to drive me there, trips were restricted to the major meetings, as I could never persuade him that anything less justified the 'long' drive from our home in Liverpool. Nevertheless, even he agreed that seeing the likes of Stirling Moss and Archie Scott Brown at the car meetings, and John Surtees and Bob McIntyre among the motorcyclists, was definitely worth it. When I was old enough and able to drive there myself, Oulton Park became a regular haunt.

The Kodak Brownie 127 camera which accompanied me was not really capable of taking acceptable action shots, and it was not until about 1964 that I acquired a viable 35mm camera. From that point onwards, photography became an integral part of every visit to the Cheshire circuit, and eventually I was able to begin contributing photographs to the weeklies, *Autosport* and *Motoring News* on a regular basis. This continued until the mid-1980s when the demands of the day job had to take precedence.

Recently I've been returning to Oulton Park; not as a photographer this time, but 'on the other side of the barriers'. For several years, I've been racing my Lotus Elan in road-sports classes, firstly with the Historic Sports Car Club, then in the Aston Martin OC's Anglo-American Challenge, and latterly in the Classic Sports Car Club's excellent Swinging Sixties races.

Throughout my years as a photographer and reporter, I happily listened to driver after driver telling me how much they liked Oulton Park, and what a great driver's circuit it was. It wasn't until I experienced it myself that I really understood what they were telling me! Oulton Park is a truly outstanding race circuit and, unlike many others, it's practically the same today as it was in the 'sixties.

My admiration for those who raced successfully on this challenging two and three quarter miles of true road circuit was high before, but is now immeasurably higher. It was impossible, of course, to include everyone but, whether they appear here or not, the pictures in this book are my small way of expressing that admiration for them all.

The author competing in his Lotus Elan in a Classic Sports Car Club Swinging Sixties Championship race at Oulton Park. Courtesy Rachel Bourne

Acknowledgements

Trawling through the many negatives and transparencies from those days has been a real pleasure, and has brought back many memories. But because the memory can play tricks, it's been an additional delight to check some of the recollections for accuracy against a number of sources, both contemporary and more recent.

Chief among these sources, of course, are *Autosport* and *Motor Sport* magazines, and the original event programmes. Books which I have found invaluable included Derek Lawson's race-by-race account of Oulton's first fifty years, *Sun, Rain ... and even Snow*, Mike Kettlewell's *Oulton Park – 25 years of car and motorcycle racing*, and Chris Ellard's *The Forgotten Races*, about the 3-litre F1 non-championship races. The two volumes of *Lotus Racing Cars* by John Tipler, and Doug Nye's books on BRM and Cooper helped shed light on individual cars, and I find G.N.Georgano's *Encyclopaedia of Motor Sport* is always a superb reference on everything up to about 1970. Any errors that remain are all mine.

Photo archive

Peter McFadyen's extensive photo archive covers racing at Aintree, Donington Park, Longridge and Oulton Park in the years 1966-1983, plus sprints, autocross, sand-racing (Southport) and occasional events at Silverstone and elsewhere. For more information, call 01386 792727 or email peter@brookhaven.co.uk

A time of change

Motor racing began at Oulton Park in August 1953 when the Mid-Cheshire Motor Club ran its first trial meeting, officially closed to the public but witnessed, nevertheless, by a crowd variously estimated at three to four thousand club members and guests. That first meeting, followed in October that year by a combined car and motorcycle meeting which attracted some 40,000 spectators from nearby Manchester, Liverpool and the north-west in general, consisted of three heats and a final for 500cc Formula 3 cars, and a 33-lap race for Formula 2 cars which was won by Tony Rolt.

At a time when Brooklands and Donington Park had been lost to motor racing as a result of war time changes, and the only alternatives were comparatively flat and uninspiring ex-airfield circuits, the emergence of something bearing a strong resemblance to a true road circuit and set in the beautiful undulating parkland which surrounded Oulton Hall was very good news indeed. The hall had been the home of the Egerton family since late in the 15th century but had been completely destroyed, first by a fire in 1926, and then, to finish the job, by two German bombs dropped in 1940. The land was commandeered by the military later that year and huts were built to house the troops. These buildings were used for a while after the war to house displaced Poles, a fact which has moved into folklore thanks largely to local personality 'Blaster' Bates' story of how Knicker Brook got its name. (If you haven't heard the story, you really should try to find a copy of his 1967 LP *Laughter with a Bang*.)

This record is still readily available via the internet.

The circuit used in 1953 turned right at The Cascades, as it was called, then right again at Range Corner, before rejoining the present circuit at Clay Hill. For the rest of its 1.5 miles it followed the layout as we know it today. In 1954, the circuit was extended in two stages to form what we would know today as the Island Circuit and then the full International Circuit, including the banked Shell (then named Esso) Bend. The British Empire Trophy came to Oulton Park in 1954, and in following years the circuit regularly hosted major sports car and Formula 1 events, and drew favourable comment from the world's top drivers and club competitors alike, who revelled in its challenging layout and attractive surroundings.

A dozen or so years after Oulton Park's birth as a racing circuit, motor racing itself was approaching a time of significant change, which would have a permanent effect on the very nature of the sport at all levels.

Sport or business?

In truth, there has probably never been such a thing as cheap motor racing. From the start, it had always been the province of wealthy individuals, whether backed by inherited money or by self-made industrial fortunes. With exceptions, such as during the politically fuelled involvement of Mercedes and Auto Union in the 1930s, it was also essentially a sport and, as such, an activity open to amateurs and individuals.

By the mid-1960s this was still largely the case. From Formula 1 to club racing, participants were virtually all self-financing, albeit with some support from companies with direct involvement in racing, such as the tyre, fuel, oil and car component manufacturers. Races were run primarily for the benefit of those taking part, and it seemed that spectators were welcome to come along if they wished. As well as watching the racing, we could easily buy reasonably priced admission to the paddock where, at close quarters, we could watch the cars being prepared and see, maybe even speak to, the drivers themselves. Formula 1 had not yet set itself apart from the rest of motor racing, and non-championship races were still a part of the calendar and enabled spectators in several countries, and especially Britain, to see Grand Prix cars and drivers competing on several different circuits during each season.

Somewhere between 1965 and 1970, it seems, that began to change. The growth of car ownership went hand-in-hand with increasing interest in motor sport, and it's not surprising that business people began to recognise an opportunity to promote all manner of products through association with it. After all, they'd been doing it in America for years. It's hardly surprising either that, with his American connections via Indianapolis and the Ford Motor Company, it would be Colin Chapman who was the first to embrace wholeheartedly the idea of sponsorship in return for marketing opportunity and to clothe his cars entirely in the corporate designs of a sponsor. Thus, the traditional Lotus colours of green and yellow, themselves something of a stylised departure from the British racing colour, would give way first to the red and gold and later black and gold of tobacco giant John Player. Compare the livery of the Lotus 33 driven by Jim Clark at the 1966 Gold Cup meeting at Oulton Park with that of the Lotus Europa of John Miles taken just two years later.

As the F1 teams became wealthier, so they sought even more money, and it was becoming increasingly difficult and expensive for organisers to gather a decent field of cars for a non-championship race. As late as 1970, the Gold Cup still attracted four World Champions in its small field, but the writing was on the wall and it wouldn't be long before contemporary works Formula 1 cars racing at Oulton Park would be but a memory.

Return of power

For the first half of the nineteen-sixties, Formula 1, the 'pinnacle of motor racing', was restricted to engines of 1.5 litres. Car designers sought to make the most of the limited power available to them by minimising

A time of change

At the 1966 Gold Cup, Jim Clark's works Lotus 33 typifies the slim, aerodynamic style of the early sixties F1 car, and still wears the British Racing Green, albeit adorned with a yellow Lotus stripe.

aerodynamic drag, leading to pencil-slim cars such as the Lotus 25 in which the driver lay almost flat in the quest to reduce the frontal area.

Meanwhile, big-engined sports cars were capturing the spectators' attention in Europe and, particularly, in North America, where CanAm was enjoying great popularity. It was essential for F1 to reassert itself at the top of the pile by adopting larger, more powerful engines. In 1966, F1 became a 3-litre formula and, three years later, following the lead of America's Formula A, Oulton Park saw the first race for Formula 5000. Power was definitely in.

Although tyre manufacturers were making ever-wider tyres in order to cope with the power being transmitted to the track, the problem remained and, as illustrated in the pages that follow, various approaches were explored. For a time, four-wheel drive seemed to offer a promising, if complicated solution, but then aerodynamic downforce

By 1968, the works Lotus Europa of John Miles is fully decked out in the livery of John Player's Gold Leaf cigarette brand.

was (re-)discovered. Initially, this meant ever more preposterous high-mounted wings, before a more sober approach, as typified by Jochen Rindt's Lotus 72C at the 1970 Gold Cup, was adopted in the wake of some catastrophic failures of these doubtful structures.

With the greater power and massively improved cornering speeds brought by these developments, there was a downside. As downforce and, therefore, grip depended upon the car's forward speed, a spinning car could lose grip and leave the track more suddenly and at much higher speed than before. This, eventually, would require changes in circuit design to maintain spectator safety. Earth banks were moved back, steel fences erected and, sadly but sensibly, some of the best spectator vantage points were closed forever in the interests of public protection. The beginnings of these changes can be seen in some of the pictures in this book, and they have gone a little further since. Thankfully, at

A time of change

By the close of the decade, we had grown accustomed to F1 cars with front and rear 'wings' and huge rear tyres to cope with their growing power outputs. This is Jochen Rindt at Old Hall during the 1970 Gold Cup race.

Oulton Park, the track itself was not as badly affected as some, and it remains to this day very little changed from its original layout. It's still one of the most – if not *the* most – picturesque race circuits in the country, and a firm favourite among all those fortunate enough to have competed on its two and three quarter miles of undulating sweeps and curves.

It's rewarding to look back, and see the way things were. For many who were there at the time, those were, indeed, the days!

Champions

Throughout the 1960s, several British circuits continued to play host to a popular but slowly vanishing form of motor sport, the non-championship Formula 1 race. Many of these took place in springtime, providing an opportunity for many of the British F1 teams and, occasionally, the Continentals to try out their new cars before the Grand Prix season proper got under way. At circuits such as Goodwood, Aintree, Silverstone and Oulton Park, these races were truly among the major events of the season in Britain.

From its inception in 1954, the Gold Cup was Oulton Park's big event of the year. Initially it was the *Daily Dispatch* Gold Cup, then the *Daily Herald* Gold Cup before becoming simply The Gold Cup. Later, as the sixties drew to a close, once more acknowledging the meeting's sponsors, it became the Guards Gold Cup.

The Gold Cup was held as a race for Formula 1 cars until 1964 when, for two years, it became a Formula 2 event, won in '64 by Jack Brabham in his 998cc Brabham BT10-Cosworth, and in '65 by reigning world champion, John Surtees at the wheel of a Lola T60-Cosworth.

In 1966, with the new 3-litre Formula 1 in place, the Gold Cup went to Jack Brabham in the Repco-engined Brabham BT19 which took him to that year's world

It was a time when even the major teams and drivers set up their base in the paddock, and took the cars to the assembly area before each race or practice session as only club racers do today. This provided spectators with an excellent opportunity to photograph the stars and their cars.

Here, on 1st April 1966, reigning World Champion Jim Clark takes his Ron Harris Team Lotus Formula 2 out for the first practice session for the following day's BARC International 200 race. When this picture was taken, it was raining, but by the following morning, Oulton Park was blanketed in snow, causing the meeting to be abandoned, and earning it the nickname 'the race that never was'.

Champions

championship. The following year saw two Formula 1 races at the Cheshire circuit, the *Daily Express* Spring Cup in April joining September's Gold Cup on the calendar. Both races fell to Jack Brabham, the first with a BT20 and the second in a BT24, both with 3-litre Repco power.

For 1968 it was back to a single F1 event, but the Gold Cup entry was one of the strongest, and included Chris Amon's works Ferrari. Jackie Stewart emerged victorious, however, in his Matra MS10-Ford. The then new Formula 5000 cars joined the F1 field for 1969's Gold Cup in August of that year, but it was the F1 Brabham BT26A-Ford driven by Jacky Ickx which took the trophy. In 1970, the last year featured in this book, the Gold Cup was again a joint F1/F5000 race, this time

held in two heats. The first was won by John Surtees in his Surtees TS7-Ford, while the second heat went to Jochen Rindt in the Gold Leaf Team Lotus 72C-Ford, the overall win going to Surtees on combined times.

Among the many other famous names who raced at Oulton Park in the period was Jim Clark, for my money the greatest driver of all and winner of the 1962 Gold Cup. Jack Brabham won four Gold Cup races, and Denny Hulme, who was very successful in sports cars at Oulton, won the 1965 Spring Cup race for Formula 2 cars. Graham Hill competed memorably in many races in Lotus and BRM cars, and over the years we were also privileged to see Bruce McLaren, Mike Spence, Innes Ireland, Jackie Oliver, Frank Gardner, Mike Hailwood, and many other top drivers of the day.

Practice days were always good for photographing drivers going about the business of preparing for the race. Here, before the 1966 Gold Cup, Jim Clark is in discussion with his mechanic and the Firestone tyre technician between practice sessions for the following day's Gold Cup race.

1966 saw the 'return to power' in Formula 1 with the new 3-litre formula replacing the previous 1½-litre limit. But suitable engines were scarce. For its Type 43, Team Lotus took on the complex H-16 BRM unit and, as it turned out, brought the engine its only Grand Prix success when Jim Clark won the US GP at the end of the season.

For the Oulton Park Gold Cup race on 17th September, Lotus entered Peter Arundell and Jim Clark in Lotus 43-BRMs, but in the end brought only one 3-litre car, for Clark. Arundell was given the interim 2-litre V8 Climax-engined Lotus 33 instead, and on the day before the race, Clark practiced in both cars.

The BRM-engined Lotus 43, seen here sweeping through Knicker Brook during the afternoon session, soon suffered engine problems causing Clark to take over the Climax car and leave Arundell a non-starter. In the race, despite a spin, Clark brought the Lotus 33 home in third place behind the Brabham-Repcos of World Champion-elect Jack Brabham and Dennis Hulme.

A bonus at non-championship F1 and F2 meetings was the chance to see the established star drivers display their talents in completely different cars in the supporting races.

After his spirited drive in the 1966 F1 Gold Cup event, Jim Clark took the wheel of his works-entered Lotus Cortina and, once Jack Oliver's Mustang had shed a front wheel and Brian Muir had put his Ford Galaxy into the Old Hall barriers, Clark completed his day's racing with yet another win. Team-mate Arundell up-ended his Lotus Cortina at Lodge but recovered to take sixth place, one lap down.

In the Formula 1 paddock of 1966, the mechanics did their work wherever they could, sometimes their only luxury being a rope to define the boundary between their workspace and the spectator area!

Here, work is in progress on the gearbox of Jackie Stewart's H-16-engined BRM after practice for the Gold Cup. The mechanical complexity so typical of BRM is clear to see.

Perhaps mindful that his mechanics were busy enough looking after the two H-16 BRMs at the 1966 Gold Cup, Jackie Stewart mans the pumps and refuels his own car prior to going out to practise.

I think this scene typifies so much of what has changed in Formula 1 since the sixties.

Stewart and team-mate Graham Hill put their cars in third and fourth places on the grid but both retired from the race.

In April 1967, the Mid-Cheshire MRC organised a special race meeting to raise funds in support of the newly instigated International Grand Prix Medical Service. There was no prize or starting money and the funds which would normally have gone to the teams were instead donated to the cause.

   With BRM supremo, Louis Stanley, as the Director General of the Service, it was natural that BRMs should be prominent in the entry for the combined Formula 1 and Formula 2 Spring Cup race.

   Jackie Stewart was back, together with new team-mate Mike Spence, and a pair of updated H-16 BRMs. Stewart took pole for Heat 1, but problems with the new mechanical fuel pump delayed him and he finished in ninth place. A great drive in Heat 2 saw him battling with Jack Brabham and coming home in fourth, 0.2s behind the Australian World Champion. An 'off' at Cascades which damaged his suspension was to put Stewart out of the final.

A BRM conference in the paddock, with BRM Chief Engineer Tony Rudd (left), Jackie Stewart and Mike Spence.

The chance to see famous racing cars from the past was an occasional bonus at Oulton Park's major meetings. Peter Collins and Tony Brooks memorably showed off the pre-war Mercedes-Benz Grand Prix cars in 1958 and, in 1967, at the Gold Cup meeting, Jackie Stewart took time off from his current H-16 F1 car to do a few stirring laps in the equally complex V16 BRM of the 1950s.

My first recollection – and photograph – of Stewart at Oulton Park was when he drove Ken Tyrell's F3 Cooper-Austin in April 1964. By 1968, he was back with Tyrell, this time driving a Matra and winning the World Championship in 1969. For the 1970 Gold Cup, Stewart was entered in Tyrell's F1 March, but the team sprang a welcome surprise by choosing the Oulton race to make its debut as a manufacturer.

Here, in the torrential rain which fell during the Friday practice session, Stewart splashes past the pits on one of the Tyrell 001's first laps in public. Teething troubles delayed the Tyrell in the following day's race before the Cosworth engine cried enough towards the end of the first heat. By this time, however, Stewart had demonstrated the potential of the new car by cutting the Oulton Park lap record to 1m 27.6s.

Another regular favourite with the Oulton Park spectators – and everywhere else – was Graham Hill, Stewart's team-mate at BRM in 1965 and 1966 when the Scot first came into F1. At the 1966 Gold Cup, the two were driving H-16 BRM P83s and, while both cars managed to hold the lead during the race, neither finished, a broken camshaft putting Hill out after an exciting race between the BRMs and the two Brabhams of Brabham and Hulme.

This picture of Hill crossing the line during the slightly damp practice session was taken from the general spectator enclosure opposite the pits, and typifies the uninterrupted view of the competing cars which was possible at the time.

Looking back over the various pictures I took of Graham Hill during the period, it seems to have been rare that he wasn't engaged in conversation with one or other of his fellow drivers. Here, at the 1966 Gold Cup meeting, he's chatting with another great character of Grand Prix racing, Innes Ireland, while spectators gather round but keep a respectful distance!

Ireland was ousted from his position as a Team Lotus driver in favour of Jim Clark, reportedly at John Surtees' behest, but not before he had had the satisfaction of becoming the first driver to win a World Championship Grand Prix at the wheel of a Lotus. At Oulton Park, Ireland was driving a privately-entered 2-litre BRM P261 which he brought home in fourth place in the race. Hill's works BRM and that of his team-mate Jackie Stewart were among the

At the 1967 Spring Cup race, Graham Hill had put on a dazzling display of how quickly a Formula 2 Lotus could lap the Oulton Park circuit, mixing it with the F1 cars and actually getting up to second place overall before engine problems intervened.

So, when the Gold Cup race later in the year looked destined to have very few F1 entries, it was opened up to F2 and an excellent entry was received in this class. Team Lotus sent along Jackie Oliver to drive a spaceframe Lotus 41, and Graham Hill with the new monocoque Type 48, seen here turning into Lodge Corner during the race. The shot was taken from the little grandstand which used to be at this spot and provided another opportunity for a close view of the cars in action.

Hill was back in a Formula 2 Lotus for the 1969 Gold Cup, this time a Type 59B with Cosworth FVA engine run for Lotus by Roy Winkelman. The race was also open to F1 and F5000 cars and Hill put on a remarkable display, passing the F5000 cars of Mike Walker, Keith Holland and Mike Hailwood. The little Lotus was up to fifth place when an oil filter seal broke, allowing the oil to leak onto the exhaust. Hill continued for several laps billowing smoke until, with four laps remaining, the oil pressure inevitably dropped and he was forced to retire.

For the 1970 Gold Cup in August of that year, Graham Hill was again Lotus mounted but now with Rob Walker's 'Brooke Bond Oxo' team's newly acquired Lotus 72 Formula 1 car. With no opportunity to drive the car before coming to Oulton, Hill – perhaps understandably – looks thoughtful after the very wet Friday afternoon practice which saw him twelfth on the grid. But he looks bright enough chatting to his fellow Lotus driver, Jochen Rindt, a few minutes later.

On the following day, Hill was to manage only four laps of the first heat before the Cosworth DFV's oil pressure dropped, and he pulled out of the race to avoid major damage to the engine.

www.veloce.co.uk
Information on all books • New book news • Special offers • Gift vouchers

Austrian Jochen Rindt was a regular visitor to Oulton, starting with the 1965 Gold Cup when he put his Roy Winkelman Racing F2 Brabham into second place on the grid but retired from the race with a broken driveshaft.

He was back for the 1967 Gold Cup which, apart from two F1 Brabhams driven by Jack Brabham and Frank Gardner, was an all F2 affair. Rindt, again driving a Winkelman entered Brabham, was third on the grid alongside his close friend Jackie Stewart (F2 Matra MS7), the pair sharing the front row with the two F1 Brabhams. In the race, the F2 field put on a tremendous dice, with Stewart eventually finishing in second overall ahead of Hill, Schlesser, Beltoise, and Rindt, who was followed home by team-mate Alan Rees.

By 1969, several F1 teams were experimenting with four-wheel drive to get the full benefit of the much greater power now available to them. Lotus introduced its Maurice Phillippe-designed Lotus 63 which Jochen Rindt refused point blank to drive because the driver's legs had to pass beneath the front driveshaft to reach the pedals (the effect of a head-on crash hardly bears thinking about). John Miles, Jo Bonnier and even Mario Andretti were brought in to drive the 63s, but eventually, at Colin

Chapman's insistence, Rindt agreed to drive the car at Oulton Park in the Gold Cup race. Team Lotus was at Oulton Park on the Thursday before the meeting to give Rindt as much time as possible to get used to the handling of the four-wheel drive car.

Before fuel pump problems sidelined him, Rindt had put the Lotus 63 into 4th place on the grid but was very late taking up his slot as the car was still being worked on in the paddock as the field assembled. Team Lotus was happy with the four-wheel drive car's progress and Rindt's second place in the race, even though he finished over a minute and a half behind the winner, Jacky Ickx in a Brabham BT26.

At the 1970 Gold Cup meeting on 21st/22nd August, Jochen Rindt was looking much happier; justifiably so as Colin Chapman had taken another giant leap forward in F1 design with the introduction of the Lotus 72. Rindt was driving the Gold Leaf Team Lotus 72C and, although hampered by the torrential rain during practice and languishing down in tenth place on the grid for Heat 1, he was soon hard on the heels of John Surtees (Surtees TS7) and Jackie Oliver (BRM P153) and finished third.

For Heat 2, with more suitable gear ratios installed, Rindt finished a clear winner, but not by a sufficient margin to prevent Surtees from taking the overall result. On his slowing down lap, Rindt stopped the car at Old Hall, collected his bag from a marshal's post, jumped into a waiting helicopter and was on his way to Vienna before Surtees had completed his slowing down lap!

No-one could have known that Rindt had just finished his last F1 race. Two weeks later, he would be practising in the same Lotus 72C for the Italian Grand Prix at Monza ...

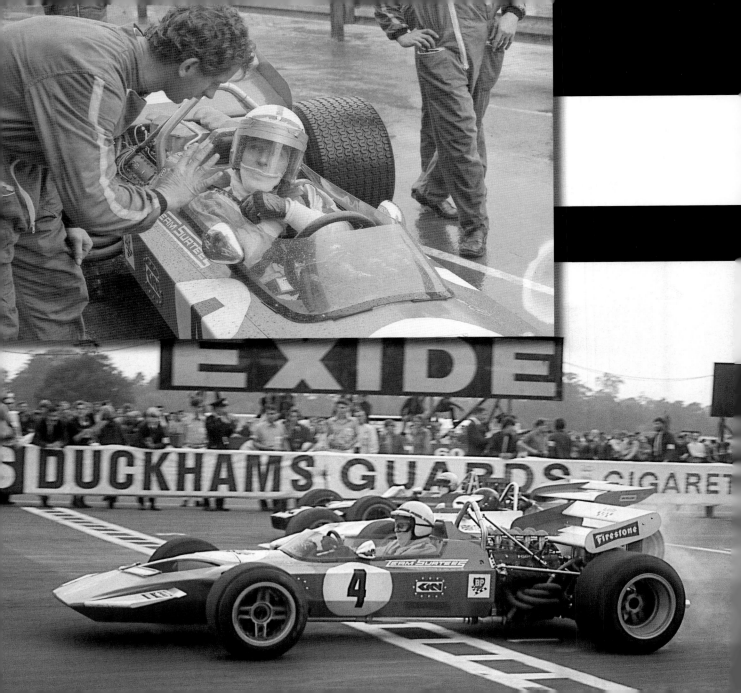

Opposite: A month after making its debut at the British Grand Prix, John Surtees' new Formula 1 car, the TS7, brought him victory in the 1970 Gold Cup. Here, during Friday's dreadfully wet practice session. he sits in the car at his pit, patiently waiting while his mechanics make further adjustments to the car. Right at the start of the session, he had been smart enough to put in some fast laps before the rain came so his pole position for the following day's race was already secure.

At the start of Heat 1, Surtees, rear tyres smoking, is already half a length ahead of the other front row occupants, Jackie Oliver (BRM) and Frank Gardner (F5000 Lola).

In 1970, pit garages weren't what they are today! BRM driver, Jackie Oliver sits on a tyre on the Oulton Park pit counter, sheltering from the rain, during practice for the 1970 Gold Cup race in which he finished third.

Champions

Australian Frank Gardner was an immensely experienced driver of all types of cars, and one who could – and still can – be relied upon to 'tell it like it is'. Here, after the 1970 Gold Cup, in which he retired from Heat 1 and won the F5000 section of Heat 2, he is about to give the circuit commentator a few well chosen words over the microphone.

As well as his development work on the Lola T190 Formula 5000 car in 1970, Frank Gardner dominated British saloon car racing in his Ford Boss 302 Mustang. Like the Lola which he had just driven in the Gold Cup race, the Mustang was entered by Motor Racing Research Ltd, and Frank concluded a successful day by winning the 19-lap race for saloon cars which ended the meeting. Brian Muir (Chevrolet Camaro) followed him home on this occasion, with Dennis Leech third in another Boss 302.

Opposite: A frequent and successful visitor to Oulton Park was Gardner's fellow Australian, Jack Brabham. Not only had Brabham won the Gold Cup in 1964 and 1966, he went on to win it twice more in 1967 and 1968. This shot of him entering Old Hall during practice for the 1967 Spring Cup – which he also won – was taken when he had recently become the first and only driver to win the World Championship at the wheel of a car bearing his own name.

Brabham was a very 'hands-on' driver, as the picture of him leaning over his Brabham BT20-Repco in the paddock clearly indicates. Although his team-mate, Dennis Hulme, won both heats of the Spring Cup race, and Brabham dropped out of the first when an ignition wire detached itself, Brabham went on to win the 30-lap final, Hulme finishing second, right behind him.

Another great Antipodean, Bruce McLaren, brought one of his own cars to Oulton Park for the first time for the 1967 Spring Cup. It was a Formula 2-based car with a 2-litre BRM V8 engine, and he finished fifth. Here, between sessions on the track, he busily signs autographs.

The top quality F2 field which appeared for the 1967 Gold Cup included Jo Schlesser driving an Ecurie Ford France-entered Matra MS5. Schlesser, who came originally from Madagascar and was twice French Formula Junior Champion, brought the car home fourth overall after a hectic dice with Graham Hill in the closing laps. Typical of the 1960s paddocks, Schlesser relaxes beside his car after practice while a young autograph hunter patiently awaits his opportunity. In the second picture, in the race, Schlesser is seen turning into Old Hall, still looking relaxed.

Sports & GT

Until 1970, there was always at least one major race at Oulton Park for sports or Grand Touring (GT) cars; starting with the British Empire Trophy, which saw victories for Alan Brown (1954), Archie Scott Brown (1955 and 1957) and Stirling Moss (1956 and 1958). The race was run at Oulton in 1959 but was just for F2 cars, although sports cars made up the rest of the programme for the meeting.

1960 was a year without top line sports and GT cars, but the Oulton Park Trophy introduced that year as an F2

event was to fill that slot for the next four years, the 1961 race for GT cars being memorable for the debut win by an E-Type Jaguar in the hands of Graham Hill. In 1962, Mike Parkes' Ferrari 250GT was victorious, and Jim Clark took the trophy in 1963 (Lotus 23B) and 1964 (2.7-litre Lotus 19) when the race was run for sports cars.

The RAC Tourist Trophy moved from Goodwood to Oulton Park in 1965 and, for the next five years, provided a feast of spectacular sports car racing at the Cheshire circuit, except for 1967 when it was held as a round of the European Touring Car Challenge. Of the four TTs held for sports cars, Denny Hulme proved his mastery by winning at the wheel of a Brabham BT8 in 1965 and in a Lola T70-Chevrolet in 1966 and 1968. The 1969 TT was won by Trevor Taylor taking the flag driving a Mk 3B Lola T70. The following year, 1970, saw no major sports car race at Oulton Park, but the British Empire Trophy made its return to the circuit, albeit as an F3 race – and a very exciting one, as we shall see.

Opposite: One of the attractions of sports car and GT races must surely be the number and variety of cars taking part. As the 1968 RAC Tourist Trophy race gets under way with 110 laps or 303.6 miles of racing ahead of them, the Lola T70s and Ford GT40s at the front of the grid are chased by Chevron B8s, Lotus Europas (including the two triple-green-striped Team Elite cars), Porsches, Costin-Nathan GT, and a Ginetta G12. Variety indeed.

Notice the relaxed attitude towards safety which, in 1968, still allowed everyone in the pits to enjoy a fine view of their car's getaway at the massed start.

Another good view could be obtained from the roof of the building which used to be right at the edge of the track at the top of Clay Hill. There wasn't a lot of room but, if you could get a place at the railing, the view down onto the cars as they swept round Knicker Brook, up the hill and on into Druids at this very fast part of the circuit was well worth the effort.

At the first meeting of the year in mid-March 1968, the Dunlop – now Yokohama – bridge, like the trees, is still in its bare winter state as David Prophet's Ford GT40 leads eventual winner, Trevor Taylor in his Lotus 47, early in the GT Championship race.

At the end of April, 1966, the RAC TT had its second running at Oulton Park and, to avoid the difficulty experienced the previous year in deciding who had won overall in a race held in two 2-hour parts, the 1966 race was to be decided over a fixed distance and run over 140 laps, although again split into two equal parts.

Denny Hulme had been given the verdict in 1965 over David Hobbs, each having won one heat and finished second in the other. This time, Hulme was in Sid Taylor's Lola T70-Chevrolet and again emerged victorious. Hulme's Brabham BT8 from 1965 was also back again, now painted red with white stripes, and was driven to second place in the second heat by Yorkshireman, Tony Dean. Here, Dean follows Peter Sutcliffe whose GT40 finished third overall and also won the Oulton Trophy for Group 6 cars. The following month, sharing the driving with Brian Redman, Sutcliffe took this car to fourth place at Spa.

In the background, cars can be seen taking the fast left-hander, Island Bend, and exiting the Esso (now Shell) hairpin.

There was only one Porsche among the entry for the 1966 Tourist Trophy, the beautiful – and very loud – Carrera 6 of Mike de Udy and Peter de Klerk. Despite gearchange problems and running for a time without rear bodywork, the car completed 131 laps and was classified sixth overall, and second among the Group 6 cars.

Ferrari was represented by David Piper's P2, Alan Rees' 275LM and Mike Parkes in a 2-litre Dino entered by Maranello Concessionaires. Here, the Dino is being pushed through the paddock with Parkes at the wheel. Transmission troubles put the car out early in the race.

Making a rare appearance at the wheel of a sports car, Jack Brabham drove his own BT17-Repco in the 1966 TT but was dogged by an oil leak which finally led to his retirement in the second part of the race. The 4.2-litre version of the Repco V8 engine used in the F1 Brabhams was brand new, and arrived from Australia only a week before the race. This picture was taken from the raised spectator enclosure at the exit of Old Hall.

At the September 1967 Gold Cup meeting, Paul Hawkins won the supporting GT race in a Ford GT40 and thereby clinched the *Autosport* GT Championship for that year. Driving the same car, the Australian was back at Oulton the following April for the Spring Cup race which, in 1968, was held for GT cars. He finished a comfortable second behind an equally comfortable winner, Brian Redman. Here, Hawkins rounds Esso Bend followed by John Bridges' Chevron B8. In the RAC Tourist Trophy that year, Hawkins was again successful in the GT40, finishing third overall.

Sadly, despite all his successes there, any mention of Paul Hawkins and Oulton Park is bound to recall the 1969 Tourist Trophy race. Practice for the race on the May Bank Holiday weekend had been marred by heavy rain, but Hawkins had put his Lola T70 on pole for the 74-lap race.

Hawkins led from the start of the race but gradually dropped back behind the similar cars of Herbert Muller (sharing with Jo Bonnier), Brian Redman and Trevor Taylor, before beginning a series of pit stops, apparently with handling problems. Rejoining well down the field, he had worked his way back up to sixth when, with the track drying after earlier rain, he came back in to change tyres on lap 65. Shortly afterwards, Hawkins' car ran wide at the very fast Island Bend, spun across the track and hit a tree, bursting into flames from which he could not be rescued. With the track blocked by wreckage, the race was stopped and

Leading the opening lap of the Guards Spring Cup race at Island Bend in April 1968 is eventual winner Brian Redman in Sidney Taylor's Lola T70 with its unpainted nose. Behind him are David Piper (Ferrari P3), Tony Dean (Ferrari Dino), Hugh Dibley in the Howmet Turbine car, and Paul Hawkins' Ford GT40.

This meeting, which also included some superb Formula 3 racing, was extremely well attended, as can be judged from the crowded slopes overlooking Cascades in the distance. Note the BBC cameraman perched atop a massive scaffolding from which he could no doubt follow the cars all the way from The Avenue, where they exited Old Hall, through the left-handers at Cascades and Island, round Esso, along the straight, through Knicker Brook and all the way up to the top of Clay Hill.

The turbine powered Howmet TX was a memorable visitor to Oulton Park in April 1968, having raced the previous week at Brands Hatch, albeit very briefly before crashing due to a jammed open throttle. It was driven, appropriately enough, by Hugh Dibley who, apart from his very successful racing career, was holding down a day job as a BOAC airline pilot.

The Howmet TX was built in America by Bob McKee for the Howmet Corporation, an organisation specialising in advanced engineering materials. The tubular chassis car, of which two were built, was powered by a Continental turbine spinning at 57,000rpm, thankfully reduced to 670rpm at the output shaft where power was rated at 330bhp. All this in a car weighing less than 650kg (1430lb). Thus equipped, the Howmet TX was classified as a Group 6 Prototype in Europe.

At Oulton Park, in the Spring Cup race, Dibley and the Howmet were going well and had covered over 70 miles before electrical problems halted their progress.

The 3-litre V8 Cosworth DFV engine which was having such success in Formula 1 came into sports car racing in 1968, powering the Alan Mann Racing Ford P68 or F3L Group 6 Prototypes. Bruce McLaren had gone well in one at Brands Hatch early in the season – until a driveshaft doughnut broke – while the two cars entered for the 1000km at the Nürburgring had fared less well, Chris Irwin crashing one of them very heavily in practice.

Richard Attwood, fresh from finishing second in the Monaco Grand Prix the week before in a BRM, was entered in the second car for the Tourist Trophy at Oulton at the beginning of June. Here he is at Old Hall on his way to putting the car into pole position ahead of Bonnier's Lola and the Ferrari P3/4 of David Piper.

Richard Attwood opposite-locking the Ford F3L through Esso during the race which he led for ten laps before retiring with a broken differential. He then went on to take over Piper's Ferrari and a share in second place overall, just ten seconds behind race winner, Denny Hulme.

And here is Hulme, the reigning World Champion, taking the flag to win his third RAC TT at Oulton Park. Practice for the bank holiday Monday race had been held on the Saturday and the 5-litre Lola T70-Chevrolet had qualified seventh in the hands of its owner and entrant, Sid Taylor, while Hulme was still travelling back from Indianapolis where, for the second time in succession, he had finished fourth. At Indy, he drove an Olsonite Eagle and, during that same year, in addition to his success with the Lola, he also won two more Grands Prix and became CanAm champion, driving for McLaren in both cases.

After his win, New Zealander Hulme removes his crash helmet and prepares to receive the Tourist Trophy for the third time, and be interviewed by commentator Anthony Marsh.

What better way to end the chapter on sports and GT races than with a picture of a Ferrari. And what better than David Piper's glorious P3/4, here in the hands of Richard Attwood in the later stages of the 1968 Tourist Trophy race in which the car finished a gallant second.

Before they were famous

A typical 'club' meeting at Oulton Park in the late sixties would attract something like 150 entries, the vast majority of which would be amateur racers simply enjoying their sport, with no expectation or even desire to progress to the higher, more professional forms of motor racing. Most had well paid jobs or careers outside motor sport; indeed, they needed a substantial income from somewhere as most paid for their racing themselves in those, largely unsponsored, days.

When, after several seasons of photography at Oulton Park, I had the opportunity to become *Autosport*'s regular photographer there, it was Simon Taylor, encouraged by the magazine's northern representative, Ian Titchmarsh, who gave me that opportunity. Simon, in truth, was already a little bit famous, as he was Assistant Editor of *Autosport*. Now, he is Chairman of Haymarket Magazines, publisher of *Autosport* and, in fact, most other UK motoring titles. He is perhaps even better known for his BBC radio commentaries on Grand Prix races, and for his excellent column in another of his publications, *Motor Sport*.

Although he didn't do a lot of racing, Simon Taylor was actually a very competent driver, and raced his own Clubmans car. In the late sixties, he was instrumental in saving this class of racing from extinction, and the Historic Clubmans series survives to this day. In March 1969, Simon was competing in the BRSCC 500 Clubmans Championship race at Oulton Park, and is seen here in the pits during practice. In the race, he was leading the 1-litre class when he spun at Knicker Brook and was hit by another competitor. Fortunately, he emerged unscathed from the overturned car.

Some would achieve fame locally at their regular circuits, while others would go virtually unnoticed except by their family and friends. A very small proportion, however, would go on to make a name for themselves within the wider world of international motor sport, whether on the track or behind the scenes as constructors, team managers, in race organisation or in what we now call 'the media'. Still fewer would go all the way as racing drivers and achieve worldwide fame and fortune at the very highest levels of the sport. Others would make it part of the way only to fade into relative obscurity later.

In this chapter, some of the now-famous names who were on the first few rungs of the ladder back in the late sixties are recalled.

David Purley, son of the LEC refrigerator magnate, is probably best remembered for surviving – just – the highest G-force ever experienced by a human being (reportedly 179.8G) when his LEC F1 car's throttle stuck open and he crashed head on at Silverstone in 1977, the car stopping from 108mph in just over half a metre (20in).

He began racing in 1968 in an AC Cobra and is seen here in a combined GT and Production Sports Car race at the BRSCC meeting on 22nd October that year. The Cobra was eventually written off and replaced by a Chevron sports car. Purley was to go on, via F3 and F2, to make his F1 debut in a March 731 at Monaco in 1973. Later, he turned to F5000 and won the 1975 Gold Cup at Oulton and the Shellsport British F5000 Championship the following year, before returning to F1 in his own Mike Pilbeam-designed F1 LEC. After Silverstone, he raced again in a second LEC F1 car and in British F1 driving a Shadow. His interest in aerobatics was to lead to his death in 1985 when his Pitts Special crashed off the south coast of England.

Future Grand Prix driver and commentator, John Watson, had been making a name for himself in his native Northern Ireland when he came to Oulton Park in October 1968 to drive a twin-cam Brabham BT16 in the mixed single seater and sports car event. He was one of several Irish drivers at the meeting and led the race initially, eventually finishing in second place. Although he did remove the Trilby for a second photograph, his team was quick to explain that "it wouldn't be John without the hat!"

In March the following year, Watson was back at Oulton, driving a Lola T-100, and lost a good third place with a spin at Esso in the opening Formule Libre race which was notable for seeing the first race appearance of the new Formula 5000 cars. Watson's career was soon taking off and he was to compete in 154 Grands Prix, winning five of them, including the 1981 British Grand Prix. After his retirement, he moved into the world of television as an accomplished and forthright commentator for Eurosport, FOCA TV and several American networks.

Another extremely successful driver now doing commentating duties in America, and who was seen in his early days at Oulton Park, is Derek Bell, seen here at the wheel of a Formula 3 Brabham BT21 on his way into Old Hall corner in October 1967. He finished second in his heat but won the final with a last second overtaking manoeuvre coming to the line.

These two cuddly chaps in the Oulton Park paddock in October 1968 are Morris 'Mo' Nunn on the left, and Australian Tim Schenken.

Schenken was coming to the end of a very successful F3 season, having already secured the Lombank F3 Championship driving the Sports Motors Chevron B9, and was about to take a very comfortable win in the day's opening race, another round of the championship.

Schenken turned to Brabham for the following year, and is seen here, during a damp practice for the Lombank F3 round which headlined Oulton's opening meeting of the 1969 season, experimenting with a high mounted wing on the BT28. The outcome must not have been too positive because the wing was removed for the race which Schenken won with ease.

Tim Schenken went on to drive for Williams, Brabham, Surtees and Trojan in F1 before turning to sports cars. In 1976, together with New Zealander Howden Ganley, he founded Tiga Racing Cars which produced over 400 cars before being sold in 1984. After running F2, F3 and even an IMSA sports car team, he turned his attentions to race organisation with CAMS (Confederation of Australian Motor Sport).

Mo Nunn began racing in 1963 and progressed to drive a Formula 3 Lotus 41, with backing from Bernard Lewis, and in 1969 drove for Team Lotus, still in F3, alongside Roy Pike.

By 1971, Nunn had become a constructor, his first Ensign F3 car scoring two wins and a second in the opening rounds of the British championship, and in 1973, Nunn's first F1 car appeared. Ensign continued in F1 until the mid-eighties when Nunn moved to America to work very successfully with the major teams, such as Newman Haas, Target Chip Gannassi, and drivers who included Emerson Fittipaldi, Jimmy Vasser.

Leicester-born Roger Williamson had been successful in karts before coming to prominence driving this 997cc Ford Anglia with great success at British circuits, including several visits to Oulton. Here he is at Old Hall in the Anglia in May 1970 when he was leading the Hepolite Glacier Special Saloon Championship overall, and scored another class win after a hectic dice with John Chappel's Mini.

With the enthusiastic backing of Donington Park owner, Tom Wheatcroft, Williamson went on to win the Lombank British F3 title in 1972, moving into F2 the following year. His introduction to F1 at the wheel of a works March 731 was brief as he was eliminated from the British Grand Prix in the first lap pile up at Woodcote, and in his next F1 race, the Dutch Grand Prix, he lost his life in a fiery accident believed to have been due to tyre failure.

The spectacular ups and downs of Tom Walkinshaw's career in the higher echelons of motor sport, culminating in the Arrows Formula 1 team debacle, have made him very famous indeed. In the late seventies, he became a very successful touring car driver, winning the European Championship among his other successes.

In 1970 he was striving to make headway in Formula 3, after winning the Scottish FF1600 championship driving a Hawke the previous year. Initially driving a Lotus, he soon moved to the March works F3 team and, at Oulton Park in early July, he finished fourth in the Lombank F3 race behind three Lotus 69s driven by Dave Walker, Carlos Pace and Bev Bond. Here, on a typical summer's day, he is seen during practice coming out of Lodge Corner in the March 703.

One up and coming driver who did make it all the way to the top, winning the world championship six years later, was James Hunt, seen here at the top of Clay Hill in his Molyslip sponsored Lotus 59. He was taking part in a round of the BOC Formule Libre Championship held on a wet day in April 1970.

A month later, he was back at Oulton in the same car for the memorable British Empire Trophy race, in the final of which he finished a very close second to Bev Bond's works Lotus 59. Here, during Heat 2, he leads Cyd Williams and Carlos Pace past the Oulton pits, in glorious Whit Monday sunshine.

Formula 5000

As it became increasingly difficult and expensive to attract Formula 1 cars to non-championship races, organisers began to look around for alternatives. John Webb, Managing Director of circuit owners Motor Circuit Developments (MCD) and the originator of the hugely successful Formula Ford series, together with Nick Syrett of the BRSCC, developed Formula 5000 for single seaters powered by production-based American V8 engines of up to five litres capacity. The idea was not completely new, however, as it was based on Formula A which had been running in America for two seasons already.

The aim was to introduce a lower-cost formula which would provide exciting, spectacular and noisy racing, and which could take the place of the disappearing Formula 1 cars at non-championship races. Formula 5000, however, was to have its own championship, the Guards European Championship.

A twelve-race series was planned for 1969, with eight of the races in the UK and four in Europe – Ireland, Holland, Belgium and Germany. The British races were to be shared between Silverstone and the four circuits owned by MCD: Brands Hatch, Snetterton, Mallory Park and Oulton Park, with the opening round scheduled for Good Friday, 4th April at Oulton Park, and the second at Brands, three days later on Easter Monday. Another of the organisers' aims was for Formula 5000 to become the highest rung on the ladder before Formula 1 itself,

and, to this end, drivers who had previously scored World Championship points were excluded.

Formula 5000 differed from the American Formula A in a number of ways, the first being that four-wheel drive, excluded in America, was permitted in F5000. This allowed David Hepworth to enter his Traco-Oldsmobile-engined Hepworth for Bev Bond to drive in the opening race. As in Formula 1, however, the incentive to suffer the added complication of four-wheel drive was eliminated when aerodynamic downforce began to solve the problem of enabling the tyres to transmit huge amounts of power to the track, so two-wheel drive remained the norm.

Secondly, the Rover 3.5-litre V8 engine was also to be permitted. It was, after all, based on a Buick engine, although it was to be the only all-aluminium engine admitted. Anticipating that full fields of 5-litre cars may not materialise at the start of the formula, for the first season only, cars powered by out-and-out racing engines of up to 2-litres were also allowed to run in the races. These cars had to weigh at least 950lb (about 432kg) while the 5-litre cars had to scale at least 1250lb (568kg). At a time when 3-litre Formula 1 cars were permitted to weigh only 500kg (plus 30kg for 'safety features' such as roll cage and safety fuel tanks), this minimum weight regulation, together with the limitations on engine modification, was to prove optimistic some of the pre-season predictions that F5000 cars would actually be faster than their Grand Prix counterparts. Nevertheless, Formula 5000 proved very successful, and certainly fulfilled its aim of providing fast and spectacular racing for the next eight seasons.

Two weeks before the opening round of the Guards Formula 5000 Championship, the two McKechnie Racing Lola T142s of Mike Walker and Doug Hardwick took the opportunity to run in the Formule Libre races at the BRSCC's Oulton Park meeting. Walker won both races, while Hardwick overcame misfiring problems in the first race to finish third in the second. Here, Walker roars out of Deer Leap on his way to his first win.

In the paddock between races, Mike Walker oversees work on the Lola, while one of his engineers takes advantage of the high rear wing. Walker's car was one of the minority which used a Bartz-tuned Chevrolet engine rather than the more popular Traco version, but he was in good company with Peter Gethin who would go on to win the championship.

Peter Gethin drove the McLaren M10A run by Bernard Hender's Church Farm Racing Team but which was effectively a works car painted in the same orange as the F1 and CanAm McLarens. His was one of two cars in the field to have fuel injection as opposed to carburettors – Andrea de Adamich's Surtees TS5 being the other – and Gethin started from the middle of the front row. When the flag dropped, Gethin went straight into the lead he was to hold throughout the race. In this shot, the McLaren is just cresting Hill Top on the run down to Knicker Brook, and some of the huge crowd (estimated at 40-50,000) which had turned out for the launch of Formula 5000, can be seen behind.

Peter Gethin, looking relaxed in the Oulton Park paddock in September at the penultimate round of the first Guards Championship season. He was well on his way to winning the Championship, but a retirement in the second 20-lap part of the race would leave him classified only in 14th place on the day.

Pipping Gethin to pole position for the inaugural F5000 race, and the only one to finish on the same lap as the winner in the race, was David Hobbs in the Len Terry-designed works Surtees TS5 powered by a Traco unit with Weber carburettors. Resplendent in red with the broad, white Surtees arrow, the car looked stunning but was causing its driver some discomfort by bottoming out in several places around the circuit. Hobbs' team-mate, de Adamich, narrowly failed to make the start when his car could not be repaired in time following an incident in practice which damaged the suspension. It had to be returned to the factory overnight for the repairs.

Mike Hailwood, many times a winner at Oulton Park in his motorcycling days, drove Paul Hawkins' Lola T142-Traco, and in the official qualifying was sliding the car around in the spectacular fashion which had been anticipated when F5000 was announced. But it seems likely that he was having to force the back end to break away in order to overcome understeer as, in the later, untimed session, with a front wing fitted to add downforce, he improved his time by 1.4 seconds. Earlier, this would have given him pole. In the race, he was well up with leaders Gethin and Hobbs when a driveshaft let go with dire consequences for the surrounding suspension.

The high-mounted rear wings sported by all the front-runners at the early F5000 races were soon to be banned as a result of the unfortunate experiences in Formula 1.

The only 2-litre car accepted for this opening F5000 race was the Team Charles Clark BRM P261 which had been raced in the Tasman Series 'down under'. Driven by Ian Mitchell, the BRM had already won a race at Oulton earlier in the season. Mitchell qualified the car ahead of several of the big cars, and was lying sixth in the race when an oil pipe burst as he arrived at the ultra-fast left-hander, Island Bend. With the front wheels well onto the grass on the inside of the bend, Mitchell fought with the car until, somehow, he managed to regain control and bring it safely to rest at Esso without any major damage.

Accelerating out of Esso against a background which clearly illustrates the parkland nature of the circuit, Mitchell's BRM is sandwiched between the two Lotus 43s of Jock Russell and Robs Lamplough. The two ex-Team Lotus cars were the ones which had originally been fitted with the BRM H-16 engines.

Russell's car was a very smart dark blue with a tartan stripe to match its driver's helmet. It had a curious mounting position for the oil coolers above the Shelby-Ford 4.7 litre engine but no rear wing. Also blue and Shelby-powered, but with a high rear wing and nose fins, Lamplough's sister car went well in practice, setting fifth fastest time, but suffered a blown engine only six laps into the race. Russell fell out a lap later with a split gearbox casing but it was great to see the two Lotuses while they lasted.

Formula 5000

By mid-September the 1969 Formula 5000 Championship was led by Peter Gethin (McLaren M10A) from Trevor Taylor (Surtees TS5) and Keith Holland (Lola T142) with Mike Hailwood still in with a mathematical chance of catching Gethin – if the top three failed to finish the last two rounds and he won both. In the event, the penultimate round, at Oulton, fell to Mike Walker with both Gethin and Taylor failing to finish the two-part race. Here, Gethin, Hailwood and Holland roar out of Old Hall in close company, their cars looking so much better without the rather ridiculous high-mounted rear wings they had carried on their first visit to the Cheshire circuit.

Trevor Taylor, the ex-works Lotus Formula 1 driver, came to the September Guards Formula 5000 Championship round having

won the previous four rounds and rapidly catching series leader Gethin. He came into the series initially when David Hobbs, like Peter Gethin, went over to the States mid-season to race in Formula A, the equivalent class there. Initially run by Team Surtees, the car, now painted white and green, was by this time being entered by Team Elite, though still with works support.

Unfortunately, the TS5, seen here hugging the inside verge at Lodge Corner, retired after only eight laps of the first heat.

In 1964, Trevor Taylor and Innes Ireland had driven a pair of BRP-BRM V8s in Formula 1 for the British Racing Partnership. The car was something of a Lotus 25 clone, but met with little success. In the Formula 5000 race at Oulton in September 1969, Kaye Griffiths entered his gold painted BRP, now fitted with 4.7-litre Ford engine, and qualified sixteenth out of 21 starters. In the race, the car lasted just seven laps before retiring at Old Hall with coolant spraying, geyser-like, from a burst pipe. The car's origin was something of a mystery but it was believed to be based on BRP chassis 2-64.

There were some big cars in Formula 5000 – and some big drivers, too. But one of the good points of the Formula was that it gave some obsolete cars a chance for a new lease of life.

This is Mike Coombe looking less than comfortable in the Cooper T66 which had been fitted with a 4.7-lite Ford engine and was known as a Cooper-Cobra. It was reportedly based on Cooper chassis number F1-2-63 which was first owned by Rob Walker and was Jo Bonnier's regular mount in 1963 Grands Prix. Later owners included Aintree Racing Team stalwarts John Scott-Davies and Jim Charnock. Coombe qualified the car at the back of the grid but finished the race in a creditable 10th place.

Good Friday in late March 1970 was one of those days when snow and hail showers came to Oulton Park, causing the Guards Formula 5000 competitors some added difficulty. The race, as before held in two 20-lap parts, was won by Mike Walker, by now driving a McLaren M10B but still entered by Alan McKechnie's organisation. The 1969 champion, Peter Gethin was back, now entered by Sid Taylor and carrying the number 1 on his McLaren M10B. Here, Walker, Gethin and Mike Hailwood approach Druids on lap two while, behind them, marshals hurry to the aid of Carlos Avallone whose Lola T140 had had an enormous accident and caught fire at Water Tower on the first lap. The Brazilian coffee man was not seriously hurt and Walker and Gethin went on to take first and second places respectively. Hailwood, however, ended his race with the Lola stuffed into the bank after an 'off' at Hill Top.

Although Formula 5000 was dominated by Lola, McLaren and Surtees, a number of other interesting cars appeared in the series. One of these was the Kitchiner K3A which appeared at the Good Friday 1970 race in the hands of Gordon Spice. Assembly of the car had been completed in the early hours of practice day, Thursday, but as yet the car did not have the benefit of the new Boss Mustang V8 engine for which it had been designed, using one of the previous year's units instead. Nevertheless, Spice finished sixth in each heat and was placed sixth overall.

Another new car at the same March 1970 race was the Leda LT20 designed by Len Terry as a development of his earlier LT17, which had been successful as the Surtees TS5. For some reason, although it looked superb, the LT20 had appalling handling and all four cars which raced in the UK were written off. This is Mac Daghorn in the pale blue and white, Bartz-Chevrolet powered car,

entered by Malaya Garages which, by this time, owned the Leda company. The picture was taken early in the first practice session before the first hailstorm struck, and before the Leda inexplicably turned sharp left at the top of Clay Hill where, of course, the cars are very light on their suspension. The car destroyed itself against the banks and barriers before coming to a halt with the driver, very fortunately, unscathed.

Although Mario Andretti had driven a Lotus 70 in a Formula A race at Sebring at the very end of 1969, retiring with engine failure while in the lead, the first appearance of the model in the UK was at Oulton Park in March 1970. Produced by Lotus Components, it was entered under Alan Rollinson's name and driven by him, and is seen here in the assembly area ready to go out for the Good Friday race.

Problems with the Vegantune Chevrolet engine during pre-race testing prevented the Lotus from getting to Oulton in time for qualifying, so Rollinson had to start from the back of the grid. The teething troubles weren't over, however, and an ignition lead came off due to bad vibration in Heat 1, and then, in the second heat, a punctured oil tank spelt the end of the Lotus 70's first F5000 race. It was, nevertheless, classified seventh out of fifteen starters.

At Brands Hatch a few days later, Rollinson was lucky to escape when, early in practice, the Lotus 70 suddenly veered off course at the very fast Hawthorn Bend and broke completely in two in the ensuing crash.

Formula 3

The need for a low-cost form of motor racing is probably as old as the sport itself. Following WWII the demand reached a new high and a new formula was introduced catering for racing cars with engines limited to 500cc. This usually meant engines from motorcycles, such as Norton and JAP. Such was its popularity that it was adopted internationally as 'Formula 3'. With large grids and close racing, it proved an ideal entry level formula and was to prove the training ground for many of Britain's future Grand Prix stars, including Stirling Moss, Peter Collins and Stuart Lewis Evans. The 500cc F3 races which often supported F1 races in Britain were frequently the best races of the day.

Although the rules have changed over the years, there has been a Formula 3 category ever since (except for a short period in the early 1960s when 'Formula Junior' took over) and it retains its fundamental role as a major step on the ladder to F1.

During its reign, the engine capacity limit for Formula Junior had been reduced from 1300cc to 1000cc, and, in 1964 a new Formula 3 was introduced with this same 1-litre limit. The age of the 'screamer' had dawned. Racing, as always in F3, was fast and furious and well supported by a mix of experienced racing drivers and talented rising stars. The use of production-based engines limited to a single carburettor, production gearboxes, and a minimum weight limit all helped to level performance between the different cars and so put a premium on driving ability. The 1-litre formula lasted until the end of the 1970 when it was replaced by one with a 1600cc limit.

There were many excellent Formula 3 races at Oulton Park during the 1-litre period but we have space here to remember only a few of them. The 1969 British Empire Trophy race was an epic among F3 races, held in two heats and a final, and demonstrated the very best of what the formula could offer.

Late October 1968, and Tony Lanfranchi in Alan Fraser's Merlyn Mk14 leads the F3 field into Lodge Corner on lap one of the day's first – and main – race. On his left is eventual winner Tim Schenken in the Sports Motors Chevron and between them Bev Bond in his Brabham BT21. Lanfranchi had the minor consolation of setting fastest lap.

This view at Oulton remains virtually unchanged to this day, give or take lots of Armco and replacement of the 'clattery' Bailey Bridge with a much more permanent-looking structure.

Taken during practice earlier on the same day with the autumn mist still reluctant to give way to the sun, this shot shows one of the two Tecno-Daf Formula 3 cars, entered by Racing Team Holland for Mike Beckwith and Gijs van Lennep, heading into Deer Leap. The cars had continuously variable ratio transmission rather than conventional gearboxes. Beckwith finished fifth while van Lennep worked his way back up to eighth after a spin at the first corner.

At the opening race meeting of 1969, eventual winner Tim Schenken in the new quasi-works Sports Motors Brabham BT28 (right) gets the drop on local driver Cyd Williams (centre) driving the Brabham entered by Natalie Goodwin and David Cole (Alexis Mk12-Cosworth) at the start of the Lombank Formula 3 race.

Lap two of the Lombank F3 race on the first Saturday of May 1969, and Roy Pike, in the very first Lotus 59, entered by Gold Leaf Team Lotus, briefly holds the lead from the Brabham BT21B of Alan Rollinson as they race out of Deer Leap. Rollinson soon took back the lead and didn't lose it again even though Pike kept up the pressure all the way to the flag.

May 1970, and a happy-looking Cyd Williams displays the trophy on his lap of honour.

Opposite: It's the final race of the 1969 season at Oulton Park and four Chevron B15s, driven by Cyd Williams, Barrie Maskell, Howden Ganley, and Richard Scott, raced wheel to wheel for the whole ten laps before Williams emerged a popular winner. Here, they sweep into Island Bend early in the race.

[Bri]tish Empire Trophy is one of Britain's oldest motor racing events, first run at Brooklands in 1932, moving to Doning[ton]
[t]hen, post-war, to the Isle of Man, before coming to Oulton Park for the first time in 1954. By then it had become
[establi]shed as a sports car race, and winners at Oulton included Archie Scott Brown and Stirling Moss. In 1959 it reverte[d to]
[bein]g an event for racing cars, and Jim Russell took the trophy driving a Formula 2 Cooper Climax. Then the race moved
[to S]ilverstone. In 1970, the British Empire Trophy returned to Oulton as a round of the *Motor Sport*/Shell Formula 3
[champ]ionship.

[The] race was held as two 10-lap heats from which thirty cars were to go forward to the 30-lap final. The heats went to T[rimm]
[er] and Cyd Williams but the final was to be an absolute cracker of a race between Bev Bond, James Hunt, and Trimme[r.]
[Bon]d, in the Lotus 59 of Gold Leaf Team Lotus, had started from the back of the grid but worked his way through the fie[ld.]
[H]e took the lead from Hunt in a daring move around the outside at Knicker Brook. Hunt and Trimmer fought back and,[as]
[t]hey are emerging from Deer Leap on the last lap with a few hundred yards to go, Bond just ahead of Hunt – also Lot[us-]
[mount]ed – and Trimmer's Brabham BT28. Gerry Birrell in the Sports Motors BT28 is in for a grandstand view of the finis[h.]

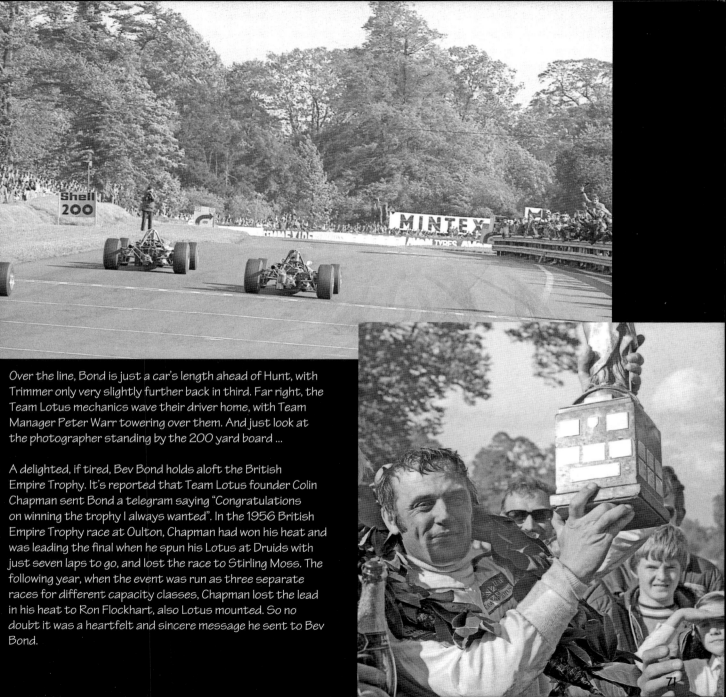

Over the line, Bond is just a car's length ahead of Hunt, with Trimmer only very slightly further back in third. Far right, the Team Lotus mechanics wave their driver home, with Team Manager Peter Warr towering over them. And just look at the photographer standing by the 200 yard board ...

A delighted, if tired, Bev Bond holds aloft the British Empire Trophy. It's reported that Team Lotus founder Colin Chapman sent Bond a telegram saying "Congratulations on winning the trophy I always wanted". In the 1956 British Empire Trophy race at Oulton, Chapman had won his heat and was leading the final when he spun his Lotus at Druids with just seven laps to go, and lost the race to Stirling Moss. The following year, when the event was run as three separate races for different capacity classes, Chapman lost the lead in his heat to Ron Flockhart, also Lotus mounted. So no doubt it was a heartfelt and sincere message he sent to Bev Bond.

Five weeks later in very different weather conditions, Bev Bond was back at Oulton, this time for a round of the Lombank Formula 3 Championship. His chisel-nosed Lotus 59 is seen throwing up the spray in front of the similar car, entered by the Jim Russell International Racing Drivers School for future Brabham Grand Prix driver, Carlos Pace.

It was Bond's Gold Leaf Team Lotus team-mate, Australian Dave Walker, who took the victory, however, and Bond dropped to third behind Pace with a spin at Esso towards the end of the race.

Old-timers

Today, historic car racing is enjoying huge popularity and vast sums of money are involved at its upper levels. Magazines and clubs have sprung up specially to cater for the growing interest, and there are historic races taking place all over the UK on just about every weekend of the season. Even the Oulton Park Gold Cup has been reincarnated in recent years and is now run as part of an historic racing 'festival' over the August bank holiday weekend. But it wasn't always this way.

In the 1960s, if you wanted to see old racing cars in action, there was just one race meeting which fitted the bill, the not to be missed Vintage Sports Car Club's Seaman Trophies Meeting held in June each year.

The VSCC was founded in 1934 to cater for cars which were at least five years old on 1st January 1935; this was later simplified to pre-1931. The founders' belief was that, with few exceptions, only cars made before this date possessed adequate performance, quality and character and so were considered to belong to a 'vintage' period in automobile history. To cater for those exceptions, they introduced the classification of Post Vintage Thoroughbred or PVT, and later were to recognise racing cars built after WWII but before 1961 as Historic, provided they were front-engined.

The VSCC's annual race commemorating the great pre-war British Grand Prix driver and Mercedes-Benz team member, Richard Seaman, was first run at Silverstone in 1950, but moved to Oulton Park in 1955 when it was won by what is probably the most famous of all ERAs, R5B or 'Remus'. Since 1963, there have been two separate Richard Seaman Trophy races at each meeting, one for Vintage cars and the other for Historic racing cars built before 1940.

Opposite top: Apart from the main Seaman Trophy races and the All-Comers or Historic Racing Car events, the VSCC's meetings are made up largely of short handicap races which allow a tremendous variety of cars, big and small, to compete together on a reasonably even footing. In one such race at the 1969 meeting, an MG leads a group of cars out of Deer Leap at the end of lap one. With many of the same cars and drivers competing year after year, their performance was always well established and the handicappers could use their knowledge to good advantage, with the result that these races became ever more exciting as the finish approached and the cars all bunched together. Roy Salvadori may have thought Goodwood on a summer's day his ideal, but the VSCC Seaman at Oulton Park on a perfect June day took some beating!

Opposite: Another view of the racing in June 1969 which, I think, typifies the vintage atmosphere; this time taken as the cars exit Druids.

Of course, the weather in June isn't always perfect. In 1968, heavy rain gave competitors in the Richard Seaman Memorial Vintage Trophy Race a chance to demonstrate their skill and bravery in adverse conditions, amply demonstrated by these two Bugatti drivers at Old Hall.

Opposite: Sometimes things do go wrong, however. At the 1970 meeting, in a 4-lap handicap for Vintage and PVT cars, EM Dean's Bugatti clipped the bank on the inside at Lodge, pitching the car into a frightening multiple roll and depositing the driver onto the track. Fortunately, it didn't land on top of him

The marshal's flags were quickly out to warn following drivers and, in the second picture, Bob Elliott-Pyle takes his Lea Francis onto the grass in avoidance, while the photographer at the extreme right is downing cameras and about to rush to the driver's

A much happier Bugatti picture – in the 1970 Seaman Historic race – one of the greatest exponents of vintage and historic racing, Neil Corner, drove this 1934 3.2-litre supercharged Bugatti entered by Sir Ralph Millais. Any notion that vintage sports car racing is about a gentle drive in the country should be dispelled by Corner's attitude in the car as he urges it through Knicker Brook on his way to second place. And remember, Knicker Brook was not a chicane in 1970; it was a very fast downhill, off-camber bend which came at the end of the fastest part of the Oulton Park circuit, the flat-out run downhill from Hill Top.

To close this section, another evocation of a perfect way to spend a Saturday afternoon as A Cherrett's 1929 Alfa Romeo 1750 leads a group of cars through Cascades in another of the VSCC's handicap races for vintage and PVT cars in 1970. It's almost as interesting to see the variety of cars in the spectator enclosure behind – Austins, Morrises, Ford Zephyr and Capri, MG, BMW, Rover – even a Volvo P1800. Old car heaven!

Left: Races for historic racing cars – pre-1961 front engined cars – were often open to 'allcomers', enabling the ERAs, etc, seen in the Seaman Historic races to have another run. However, these races were dominated by Grand Prix cars of the 1950s, such as Maserati 250Fs, Connaughts, Cooper Bristols, and even an occasional Ferrari. The Lotus 16-Climax of the late 1950s was a fragile car in its day, but in historic racing has proved fast and much more reliable, albeit in shorter races. This is Bill Wilks' car driven by C Lucas at the 1970 Seaman meeting, seen against the equally

Images of Oulton

In any given season, Oulton Park would host two, maybe three, major race meetings. The Gold Cup, the Tourist Trophy and the Easter, usually Good Friday, race meeting. For many, the VSCC's Seaman Trophies meeting for Vintage and Historic cars was a highlight of the summer.

On a dozen or so other weekends between March and October, the Cheshire parkland circuit was home to some of the best 'club' racing in the country. National clubs, such as the British Racing & Sports Car Club (BRSCC) and British Automobile Racing Club (BARC) shared the calendar with local clubs, notably the Mid-Cheshire Motor Racing Club and the Lancashire & Cheshire Car Club, whilst others, such as the Chester Motor Club would contribute perhaps one meeting per season. Races catered for saloon cars, sports cars, and a variety of single-seater classes, with Formula Ford becoming a regular feature from its introduction in 1967. Often, there would be one or more allcomers or Formule Libre races, open to any type of car, closed or open wheel – not something we're likely to see today.

For many drivers, Oulton Park was their local circuit, for others it soon became a favourite, and they would return over and over again building up a following among the regular spectators and becoming something of local heroes or, at the very least, familiar faces. The cars seen at these Oulton meetings were mostly typical club racers, with Minis, Ford Anglias and Cortinas proliferating in the saloon classes, and Lotus Elans and Jaguar E-Types in the sports car races. It was not uncommon to see more exotic cars, such as a Ford GT40, AC Cobra or Ferrari LM in there with them.

And then, of course, there were the Chevrons, for whom it was effectively their local circuit. These beautiful and charismatic cars were popular with local drivers and spectators alike, and many a Chevron made the short trip from Bolton to Oulton for its first race.

In this chapter, just a few of the scenes of club racing at Oulton Park in the late 'sixties are recalled, hopefully giving a flavour of those times and perhaps evoking a memory or two of days and drivers gone by.

Opposite top: Encapsulating much of the relaxed atmosphere of a typical Oulton Park 'Clubbie', the start of this Formule Libre race at the Lancashire & Cheshire Car Club's meeting on Whit Saturday, May 1966, has Jim Charnock (Cooper) on pole, John Scott-Davies in his Lotus 19 sports car, and John Bridges in his Brabham on the outside of the front row. The Chevron B2s of Don Hill and John Carden, Derek Walker's yellow Ladybird, and Brian Toft's blue and yellow Anco Monoposto share the next two rows with a Cooper and a Lotus 18, while a Lotus 7 driver, with a novice's cross on the rear of his car, raises his hand to signal a dead engine. Notice the rather rickety rostrum which looks to be in danger of collapsing beneath the brave starter who has just dropped the Union Jack to unleash the field.

Opposite bottom: Spectators had a close-up and unobstructed view of the action at Old Hall, as illustrated in this shot of the tyre-smoking Minis of Barry Pearson and R Cluley who finished first and second in the 1001-1300cc class of the Peco Trophy

Another good place to watch was from was the stand at Lodge where cars approached directly towards the spectators on the run from Druids before, hopefully, turning right. According to Barrie 'Whizzo' Williams, drivers could see the whites of the spectators' eyes on the approach. The cue to brake was when their mouths opened! The stand is no longer there, of course.

Martin Birrane's Ford Falcon uses all the road plus a bit as it scrabbles its way back onto the track, and George Whitehead's WRA Anglia continues on its way in June 1969.

There was another small grandstand at Lodge Corner, of course, also now but a memory. It was on the approach to the corner, and afforded a very close view of the action. It can be seen in the background as the great Gerry Marshall opposite-locks the Shaw and Kilburn Vauxhall Viva through Lodge ahead of R J Jones' Mark II Cortina Lotus in April 1969.

Much of what has changed at Oulton Park has been for the good, of course. Awaiting the unwary on the outside of Knicker Brook, for example, used to be a drop into something resembling a swamp. This has long since been filled in and levelled over.

In April 1966, John Scott-Davies' E-Type strayed over the edge and landed upside down where it was left for the rest of the meeting! Scott-Davies escaped unharmed, and that's him passing by in his Lotus 19 during the Formule Libre race.

Left: Tragically, a local driver who had rapidly become a favourite with the Oulton spectators was less fortunate. Stuart Howitt, or Stu-itt as one commentator called him, was the son of a Liverpool road transport company proprietor and was making a name for himself with his successes at the wheel of his Fraser Imp, especially at Oulton Park. This shot was taken as he exited Lodge in November 1967.

The following June, on the opening lap of a saloon car race, Stuart's Imp ran a little wide at Knicker Brook and the car toppled down the bank. What should have been no more than a racing incident turned to tragedy as he was trapped in the car, under the water, and the marshals could not get to him in time to save his life.

On a much happier note, here is David Prophet's gorgeous Ferrari 275LM at the BARC 'club' meeting in March 1967. Think about it; only two years earlier this type of car – the NART 250LM driven by Masten Gregory and Jochen Rindt – had won the Le Mans 24 Hours. It's like seeing a Bentley Speed 8 racing in a 2006 'Clubbie'. Not only that, Prophet didn't win but finished behind another supercar, John Harris' Ford GT40.

In July 1966, having had his second ever single-seater race earlier in the day, driving John Bridges' Brabham BT14 to second place behind Robin Darlington's Kincraft, Brian Redman then turned to the Red Rose Motors Lola T70 and took a resounding win in the Formule Libre race.

Redman was very much a favourite at Oulton Park, and his association with Bridges' Red Rose team first enabled him to demonstrate his talent when he drove Charles Bridges' lightweight E-Type. He had a long and close association with Chevron, helping win the European 2-litre Sports Car Championship in 1970, as well as winning at Oulton Park in a Formula 5000 Chevron B24. Redman is known as an extremely successful sports car driver, and also drove in Formula 1, finishing third in the Spanish GP only two years after this picture was taken.

John Bridges was a familiar sight to Oulton Park spectators in the 60s, and he was definitely a local favourite having taken over his brother Charles' Red Rose Motors garage business in nearby Chester in 1968. About the same time, John became a director and shareholder of Derek Bennett Engineering, the company responsible for those other Oulton favourites, Chevrons. It is said that the 'B' in the Chevron type numbers stood for Bridges, not Bennett.

John Bridges' Chevron B8-BMW is seen at Old Hall on 15th June 1968 when he won two races.

The man responsible for designing the successful Chevron cars, Derek Bennett, was also a very capable racing driver. He was entered in one of his Chevron B8s for the RAC Tourist Trophy race at Oulton Park in June 1968, sharing the Tech-Speed car with Alan Rollinson. Bennett, seen here turning into Cascades, set the car's qualifying time, but throttle linkage problems were to put the car out of the race before he was able to take over from Rollinson.

One of the earliest Chevrons, a B2 Clubman, was campaigned very successfully for a number of years by Dave Rees who is seen here looking very relaxed and in control as he goes on his way to another Oulton Park win in April 1970.

No, not a one-make race, but an illustration of just how popular and successful were the Chevron B8s in sports and GT races. At this point in the race, as the four leaders sweep over the top of Clay Hill, Jeff Hodgson has the lead from Trevor Twaites, eventual winner John Bridges and Phil Silverston. The picture was taken on 22nd March 1969.

A firm local favourite was Natalie Goodwin who raced her black Lotus 7 with great success. Natalie had a habit of holding on to the side of the car in corners, as here at Old Hall, something many 500cc F3 drivers also seemed to do. She went on to race a Formula 3 Brabham, and also entered the very successful Cyd Williams car in Formula 3.

Doncaster driver, Tony Sugden could hardly be described as local, but he raced so often at Oulton Park that it felt as though he was. In fact, Tony raced all over the country, and very successfully, starting out in the 2-litre Ford Escort seen here. In later years, he was to drive a Chevron B23 sports car in Formule Libre races before converting the car into a Skoda Special Saloon Car, which he continued to race for many years.

Alongside Tony in this picture is another prolific racer, John Myerscough, the Bolton driver who had his first race at Oulton Park in a Mini in 1966. From the Westune Anglia, John went on to drive the ex-Mike Walker McLaren M10B in F5000 races, followed by many more years of successful saloon car racing, including the BTCC in 1978.

No book on Oulton Park would be complete without Derek Walker, the market gardener from Hale, Cheshire. In the first 25 years of racing at Oulton Park, Derek was to be the circuit's most successful driver, with 37 wins between 1961 and 1977. This feat is all the more remarkable for the fact that he also built his own cars, calling each one Ladybird, this being the Mark X Ladybird on its first outing in March 1970 when it finished third. Having started with cars for the Clubmans-style 1172 Formula, he went on to Formula Ford versions before turning to Special Saloons, again all self-designed and built. Derek is still racing regularly and successfully in Historic Formula Junior with a Terrier Mk4, and is rarely challenged in the front-engined class.

The Chevron B8s of Trevor Twaites and Phil
Silverston head out of Deer Leap on their
way to start another lap of Oulton Park.

Also from Veloce Publishing –

ISBN – 1-903706-01-7 – £9.99

ISBN – 1-903706-81-5 – £9.99

ISBN – 1-903706-49-1 – £12.99

ISBN – 1-903706-79-3 – £9.99

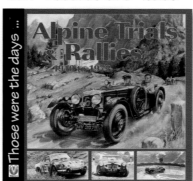

ISBN – 1-904788-95-5 – £12.99

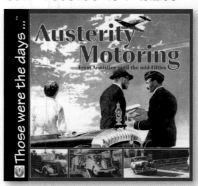

ISBN – 1-903706-86-6 – £9.99

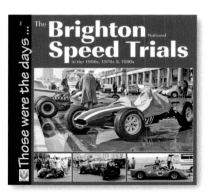

ISBN – 1-903706-88-2 – £12.99

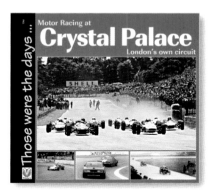

ISBN – 1-904788-34-3 – £12.99

ISBN – 1-904788-06-8 – £12.99

ISBN – 1-904788-66-1 – £12.99

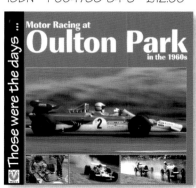

ISBN – 1-84584-038-0 – £12.99

Note: All prices exclude P&P. See our website or call +1305 260068 or email info@veloce.co.uk for more information.

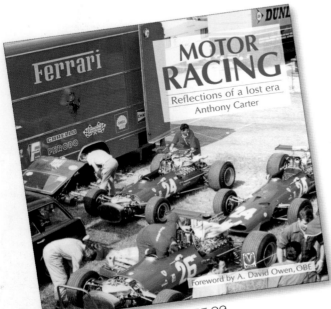

ISBN – 1-904788-10-6 – £35.99

ISBN – 1-904788-15-7 – £29.99

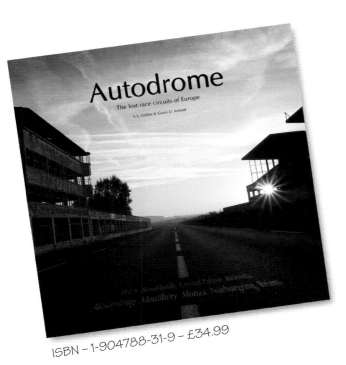

ISBN – 1-904788-31-9 – £34.99

ISBN – 1-84584-016-X – £39.99

Note: All prices exclude P&P. See our website or call +1305 260068 or email info@veloce.co.uk for more information.

Index